SUNSHINE *from* DARKNESS

THE OTHER SIDE OF OUTSIDER ART

ARTISTS REACHING BEYOND THE STIGMA OF MENTAL ILLNESS

Front Cover Art by: Aranda Michaels. *Mount Hood.* Watercolor and Ink, 9 x 12"

SUNSHINE *from* DARKNESS

THE OTHER SIDE OF OUTSIDER ART

ARTISTS REACHING BEYOND THE STIGMA OF MENTAL ILLNESS

NANCY GLIDDEN SMITH

NARSAD Artworks • Brea, California

NARSAD Artworks wishes to express its gratitude to

 · PHARMACEUTICA ·
· RESEARCH FOUNDATION ·

for making this book possible through a generous educational grant.

Photo Credits:

RUTH MC DOWELL photo on page 8 by
Bob Ross, R.A.R.E. Photography, Albany, Oregon

ROSEMARY OTTO photo on page 20 by
Robert Marsh, Lake Worth, Florida

KEVIN LONGINI photo on page 26 by
Georgia Longini, Mill Valley, California

AARON HOLLIDAY photo on page 30,
LA RUE ALEGRIA photo on page 48,
MICHAEL KORT photo on page 66, and
CATHERINE BROGER photo on page 96 by
Steve Burns Photography, Whittier, California

JENNIE LYNN JAMISON photo on page 54 by
Dustin Peck, KPC Photography, Charlotte, North Carolina

TOM WAGNER photo on page 57 by
Mark Cohen, Wilkes-Barre, Pennsylvania

ARANDA MICHAELS photo on page 78 by
Murray and Lapp Photographers, Portland, Oregon

ERIC PETERSEN photo on page 88 by
Dennis Keim, Eugene, Oregon

MARK BISHOP photo on page 102 by
Michael Bishop, Clackamas, Oregon

SUZANNE RICH photo on page 106 by
Stephen Brusius, Oshkosh, Wisconsin

Editorial Assistance:
Hal Hollister, Patsy Hollister, Joan Tani, and Renee Tawa

Printing:
Advance Color Graphics, Buena Park, California

Design and Layout:
Gordon Tani, Tani Design & Advertising, Cerritos, California

Library of Congress Catalog Card Number: 97-91566

First Edition, May 1997

Library of Congress Cataloging-in-Publication Data

Smith, Nancy Glidden.
Sunshine from Darkness: The Other Side of Outsider Art
ISBN 0-9657950-0-4

TABLE OF CONTENTS

Aaron Holliday. *Spring Garden.* Oil, 40 x 30"

Aranda Michaels. *To Bring.* Watercolor, 9 x 7"

Mark Bishop. *Man With Beard.* Pastel, 15¹/₂ x 12"

La Rue Alegria, *Golden Glory.* Watercolor, 23 x 17³/₄"

"The more I am spent, ill, a broken pitcher," wrote Vincent van Gogh, "by so much more am I an artist." And, certainly, van Gogh's life and art bear strong witness to the complicated, intriguing, and controversial link between mental illness and artistic creation. The increasingly well-documented association between some forms of psychopathology, especially depression and manic-depressive illness, and creativity remains a source of fierce dispute within certain quarters. Some artists and art critics, for instance, find it a reductionist concept, a perpetuation of a damaging "mad genius" stereotype. Others, advocates for the mentally ill, occasionally decry the hypothesized link as a seeming romantization of painful, costly, and frequently lethal illnesses.

That there have been many outstanding artists and sculptors who have suffered from mental illness is unquestionable. A partial listing would include Ralph Blakelock, David Bomberg, John Sell Cotman, Richard Dadd, Thomas Eakins, Paul Gauguin, Théodore Géricault, Hugo van der Goes, Philip Guston, Carl Hill, Ernst Josephson, George Innes, Edwin Landseer, Edward Lear, John Martin, Charles Méryon, Michelangelo, Adolphe Monticelli, Georgia O'Keefe, Raphaelle Peale, Jackson Pollock, George Romney, Dante Gabriel Rossetti, George Frederic Watts, Sir David Wilkie, and Anders Zorn. Many others committed suicide: Ralph Barton, Francesco Bassano, Francesco Borromini, Edward Dayes, Vincent van Gogh, Arshile Gorky, Benjamin Haydon, Ernst Ludwig Kirchner, Wilhelm Lehmbruck, Jules Pascin, Mark Rothko, Nicholas de Staël, Pietro Testa, and Henry Tilson.

That so many individual lives were destroyed, overshadowed, or prematurely ended by suicide is, of course, compelling in a deeply human sense. It does not, however, prove a link between mental illness and great achievement in the arts. The link, to the extent that it exists, has been more persuasively demonstrated by a score of scientific and biographical studies completed during the past twenty years, virtually all of which have found a striking and quite consistently disproportionate rate of severe mood disorders in artists and writers. The many explanations for this association between mental illness and artistic creativity have focused upon temperament, motivation, cognitive changes that occur during altered mood states, visionary and ecstatic states, intensity and range of emotional experiences, and perspectives gleaned from painful events and emotions.

The artwork in this book reflects the lives, experiences, and talents of less well known artists, artists whose mental illness, vision, and ability have informed their work in meaningful ways. Their art reflects the diversity of the human experience. The discipline of their art, as well as its expressiveness, can be seen in the variety and beauty of the work found in these pages. Far from being the stereotypic "work of the mad", the drawings and paintings in this book demonstrate the essential combination of discipline, emotion, and imagination that comprises the basis of creative work.

Kay Redfield Jamison
Professor of Psychiatry
The Johns Hopkins School of Medicine

Darkness descended on Annick Hollister at 15, when she was the picture postcard Southern California girl – blonde, blue eyes, leggy, and tan. She was a track star and a top student. And she was sophomore class vice president for a day before her world turned upside down in 1978. She began having visions. She saw God in the setting sun on the California shore. She ran away from home and kept running across the United States, to Tijuana, anywhere, nowhere, searching for nirvana. As Annick's agonized family searched for answers, psychiatrists put a name to her bizarre behavior: schizophrenia.

Self-Portrait. Watercolor, 17 x 14"

For the next ten years, the darkness was almost unremitting. But always, there was one ray of light. Even in those tortured years, Annick still turned to art for solace, as she had done since she was 3. Art was a way for her to express herself when words were not enough. Annick's parents, Patsy and Hal Hollister, clung to her art as a glimmer of hope during the years of hopelessness. "How," they asked each other, "can we use Annick's art to help her?" And later: "How can the art of any person stricken by a mental illness be used to help all who thus suffer?"

That was the genesis of NARSAD Artworks, a Southern California-based offshoot of the National Alliance for Research on Schizophrenia and Depression. NARSAD Artworks is an all-volunteer nonprofit corporation which uses art created by persons with mental illness in products such as note and holiday cards sold nationally to educate the public, to provide support for the artists and to raise money for causes related to brain disorders, especially research.

Patsy came up with the "Sunshine from Darkness" theme, based on one of Annick's early paintings, a stairway rising from darkness. That phrase has been used on our Mental Illness Awareness posters each October since 1989. Other notable works by Annick include "White Cat" which adorned our first poster, and

Out of Darkness. Watercolor, 11 x 14"

Yellow Sailboats. Watercolor, 9 x 12"

"Yellow Sailboats," one in a series of eight that Annick painted while in the acute ward of a major state hospital. "I was able to block out the demons while concentrating on the detail of those pictures," Annick remembers. Her work is broad in scope: She completed a self-portrait in 1988, a year before she began a successful regime of new medication. And in 1992, she painted the jubilant and whimsical "A Gathering of Friends."

We believe we are the nation's largest recipient of art created by persons with severe mental illnesses. Very little of what we receive shows any of the disturbed quality or abberance so often associated with so-called "outsider art." Instead, our artists simply produce quality, well-executed original art by any standard. Thus the reason for our subtitle, "The Other Side of Outsider Art."

Of special note has been the wonderful assistance of Nancy Smith who has no direct connection with mental illness but, from the beginning, has coordinated all communications and dealings with our artists. "Sunshine from Darkness – The Other Side of Outsider Art" would never have become a reality without her. Every page has her caring imprint.

Patsy and Hal Hollister, NARSAD Artworks founders, Brea, California, 1997

White Cat. Watercolor, 13³/₄ x 10¹/₂"

A Gathering of Friends. Watercolor, 9 x 12"

We dedicate this book to Annick, who is now 35, for she was the inspiration for NARSAD Artworks. Because of her, hundreds of artists with mental illness are gaining recognition and being accepted for their abilities rather than their disabilities. We are proud to present 18 of these accomplished artists in this book.

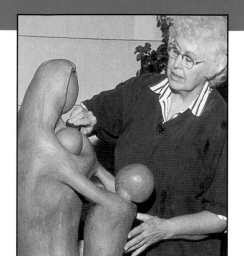

Born May 18, 1927

Ruth is such an accomplished artist that private collectors snap up her work. She wanted to draw as soon as she could hold a pencil, starting out with cartoons of her siblings. Even when she worked as a nurse for twenty years, from 1961 through 1979, she took one class a week. She started out with abstracts in her classes and then switched to watercolors in 1978. In the early 1980's she studied wheel throwing and hand forming along with the chemistry of glazes and salt firing. Ruth is a widow and mother of two children and four grandchildren.

Pink Iris. Watercolor, 30 x 20"

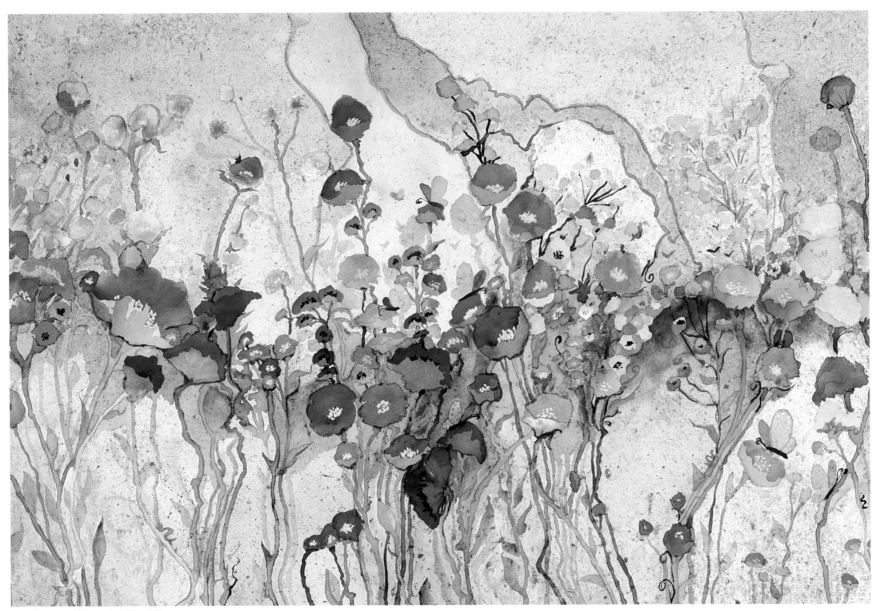

Floral Fantasy. Watercolor, 22 x 30"

Musical Fantasy. Watercolor, 30 x 22"

Flowering Plum. Watercolor, 22 x 30"

African Gladiolus. Watercolor, 30 x 22"

Thistle. Watercolor, 30 x 22"

Stormy Landscape. Watercolor, 22 x 30"

Flowering Blackberry. Watercolor, 22 x 30"

Blackberry Vine. Watercolor, 30 x 22"

"I have mild bi-polar affective disorder. Being an artist gives me pleasure and a feeling of accomplishment. I have a need to be productive."

Kay's Daisies. Watercolor, 22 x 30"

Queen Anne's Lace. Watercolor, 22 x 30"

Waltz. Pit Fired Ceramic, 15 x 15"

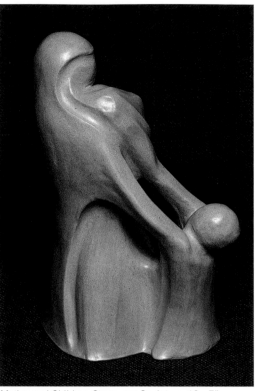

Mother and Children. Stoneware Sculpture, 12 x 7"

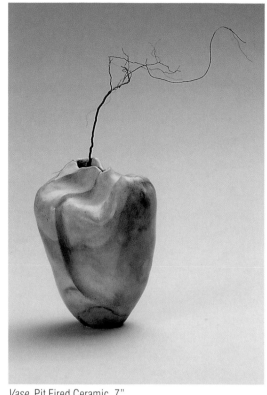

Vase. Pit Fired Ceramic, 7"

My Life Is Full. Pit Fired Ceramic, 5"

"I feel more at home with hand forming and at present I am finishing a 29" stoneware piece similar to the small piece that was presented to Tipper Gore by Bazelon Center for Mental Health Law to honor Mrs. Gore for her leadership in erasing the stigma of mental illness."

Few artists get their own shows, but Abe did – at the tender age of 14. His first show in Maryland included 30 pieces in pastel, ink, pencil and oils. He went on to study art at Howard Community College and graduated with an AA degree. Now he is a senior at the University of Maryland, where he is pursuing a BA degree in psychology. Abe is fascinated with wild animals and spends time sketching at the zoo. He has an amazing ability to capture the essence of the animal through the expression in the eyes. Before being diagnosed with schizophrenia, Abe was a star soccer player and still has a keen interest in the sport.

Born August 12, 1970

"I have always been interested in art. I seem to have an innate talent which flourished during middle school."

Lion in the Breeze. Acrylic, 21 x 27"

Fox. Pastel, 17¹/₂ x 12"

"My special interest is the realistic portrayal of animals. The medium best suited for this, in my opinion, is pastel."

Deer. Pastel, 16 x 11¹/₂"

Black Panther. Pastel, 19³/₄ x 24"

Born November 16, 1938

The ocean has beckoned Rosemary since she was a child. Ocean scenes play a prominent role in most of her paintings. While a child in Germany during the second world war, she received a set of crayons from her artist mother. Rosemary was used to dark colors so the bright colors impressed her with their beauty. She returned to the United States and her first breakdown occurred at age 19. She has had three major setbacks since, one of which resulted in a three year hospital stay. At first she hated the hospital but the people helped her think of it as home. In the hospital she turned to oil painting and fell in love with that medium. Now Rosemary creates unique primitive triptychs with vibrant colors which, along with her etchings, engravings and paintings, have been in numerous galleries in Florida where she has lived for many years.

The Oil Painted Collage medium which Rosemary has developed is unique and is an adaptation of the collagraph printing technique using rag paper instead of canvas.

Unicorn. Mixed Media, Triptych, 20 x 32"

Circus. Mixed Media, Triptych, 18 x 24"

Deer People. Oil, 16 x 20"

"The ocean symbolizes the stream of consciousness."

South Ocean. Oil, 24 x 30"

Strangers and Others. Oil, 60 x 48"

"My art is allegorical."

Mermaid. Watercolor, 24 x 18"

26

Virgin and Babe. Mixed Media, Triptych, 14 x 23"

Blue Horse. Watercolor, 18 x 24"

Born January 4, 1950

Kevin was a remarkably bright child. His parents knew immediately that he was special. He began drawing at age three. He walked at the age of six months and at an early age tested as genius. At age five on a visit to Mexico City, he fell in love with the country's art and immediately set out to create paintings of his own. By age seven he was so accomplished his own mother mistook his work for a professional. When an artist friend visited their home, Kevin's mother complimented the artist on his work and the artist replied, "These are not mine, they are Kevin's." Kevin grew up in Marin County, California. He studied art in high school and graduated from the local college with an AA in art. Now he paints sporadically and primarily works with mixed media, such as tissue paper and ink.

"Art is the biggest part of my life."

Mark's Last Hurdle.
Mixed Media, 37$\frac{1}{2}$ x 25"

The Break-Up. Mixed Media, 24 x 24"

Love is like a bird,
Like a robin on the
first breath of spring.
It's here for awhile,
and then you see it,
enjoy it, love it....
And then it's gone,
with the first breath of
winter, not realizing
All the springs beyond.
– Kevin Longini

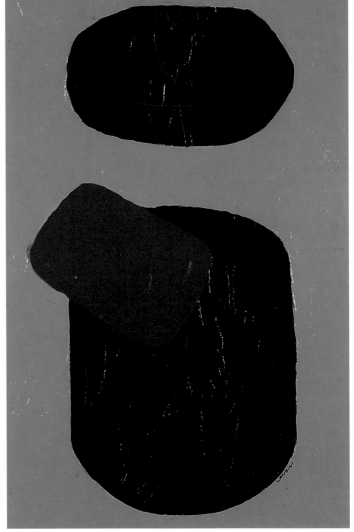

Untitled. Mixed Media, 36 x 24"

"I often have 'artist's block,' much like a writer, which is why I paint sporadically, but there are times when once I begin, I don't stop."

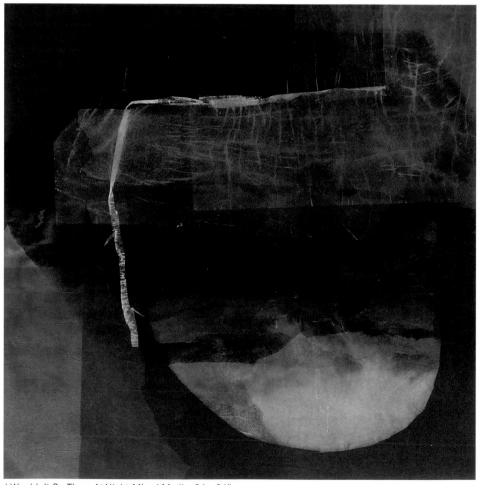

In the Creek. Mixed Media, 36 x 24"

I Wouldn't Go There At Night. Mixed Media, 24 x 24"

"Art gives me a different perception
of my own life."

Untitled. Mixed Media, 20 x 16"

31

Born May 16, 1948

At age 13 Aaron's artwork brought him solace from the loneliness he felt growing up in Los Angeles even though he came from a large family. He was raised by his grandmother who had her hands full trying to keep the family together. He gradually withdrew from people and was so obsessed with drawing that he wouldn't come out of his room to go to school and was hospitalized for three years. Aaron is self-taught and his oil paintings are masterpieces of color and composition. His pencil drawings are enchanting. Aaron is fond of drawing mermaids and mermen and he does not "humanize" them. His mermaids have gills instead of ears. The Indian and Japanese themes express his extraordinary imagination. Aaron continues to spend much of his time drawing or painting.

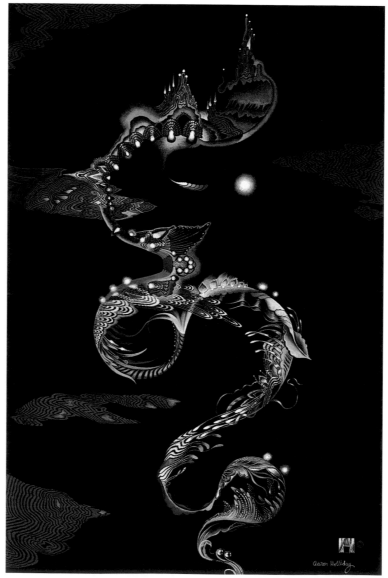

Fascination. Oil, 36 x 24"

"In my lonely state as a child I would lie awake in bed and could visualize a golden dancing globe of light moving from right to left, creating lights and shapes of all colors. As I grew older, everything I visualized became smaller and now they no longer appear."

Dancing on the Wind. Oil, 40 x 30"

Rhapsody. Oil, 40 x 30"

Feathered Hunter. Colored Pencil, 24 x 19"

Stream of Time. Oil, 40 x 30"

Prince Shermann. Oil, 40 x 40"

Birds. Oil, 40 x 30"

Crystal House. Oil, 40 x 30"

Antique Shop. Oil, 40 x 30"

Lady of the Leaves. Oil, 40 x 30"

Lady of Tears. Pencil, 24 x 19"

Emperor of the Valley. Pencil, 28 x 22"

"I have stories called 'Tales of the Golden Eagles' telling of many adventures."

Night Riders. Pencil, 28 x 22"

Winged Rider. Pencil, 22 x 28"

"Three Golden Butterflies' is my story of a Japanese version of the King Midas fairy tale."

Ladies of the Golden Butterflies. Pencil, 28 x 22"

Underwater Adversary. Pencil, 28 x 22"

Water Maiden. Pencil, 28 x 22"

Summer Garden. Pencil, 28 x 22"

44

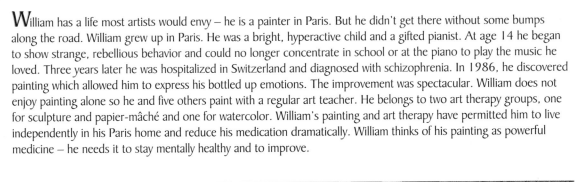

William has a life most artists would envy – he is a painter in Paris. But he didn't get there without some bumps along the road. William grew up in Paris. He was a bright, hyperactive child and a gifted pianist. At age 14 he began to show strange, rebellious behavior and could no longer concentrate in school or at the piano to play the music he loved. Three years later he was hospitalized in Switzerland and diagnosed with schizophrenia. In 1986, he discovered painting which allowed him to express his bottled up emotions. The improvement was spectacular. William does not enjoy painting alone so he and five others paint with a regular art teacher. He belongs to two art therapy groups, one for sculpture and papier-mâché and one for watercolor. William's painting and art therapy have permitted him to live independently in his Paris home and reduce his medication dramatically. William thinks of his painting as powerful medicine – he needs it to stay mentally healthy and to improve.

Born in Paris, September 28, 1955

Calla Lilies. Acrylic, 32 x 23¹/₂"

La Femme Fauve. Acrylic, 45 x 35"

French Landscape. Acrylic, 26 x 32"

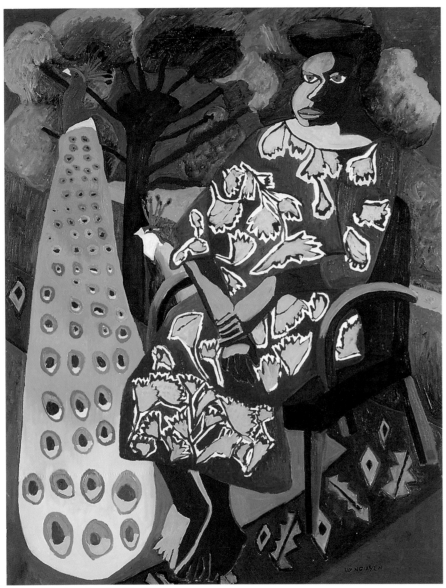

African Priestess. Acrylic, 45 x 35"

Still Life. Acrylic, 12 x 17½"

River in Auvergne. Acrylic, 36 x 28³/₄"

Lions. Acrylic, 19¹/₂ x 24"

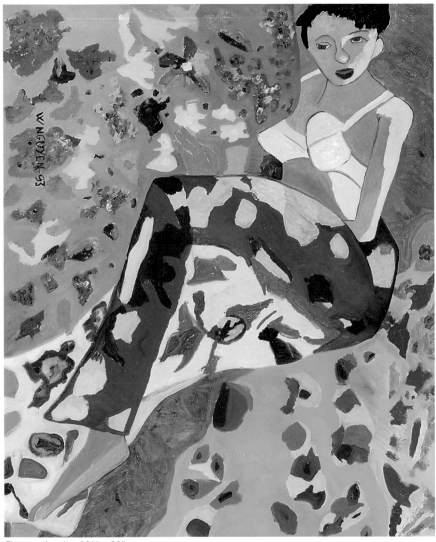

Flowers. Acrylic, 39¹/₂ x 32"

Bottles. Acrylic, 24 x 19¹/₂"

Born December 11, 1947

As a child La Rue's eyes were always drawn to color, the bright colors in her mother's and grandmother's quilts, the red and green lights on the Christmas tree. This passion for color was profoundly enhanced by living in a very sterile, stark housing project environment (old military housing) where every room was painted institutional green. La Rue began painting at the age of 19, as a young mother, after her three children were asleep. Into the night, she painted vivid landscapes and still lifes in brilliant hues of blue, gold and red-orange – finally in touch with the beloved colors that had escaped her for so many years. Her work is important therapy in her ongoing recovery from bi-polar disorder.

Self-Portrait. Watercolor, 18 x 23"

Binary System. Watercolor, 30 x 22"

Untitled. Mixed Media, 24 x 20"

Jester. Watercolor, 17¹/₄ x 23¹/₂"

Dysfunctional Functionals. Watercolor, 18 x 24"

"The creative process has given me an awesome outlet for expression of moods through color, shape, and composition."

Untitled. Watercolor, 21 x 26"

"Among my mentors is my artistic older sister. She suffers from schizophrenia as does her son and my son. I paint for them and for all who suffer from bio-chemical imbalances of the brain."

Tulips. Watercolor, 24 x 18"

Elements. Watercolor, 24 x 18"

"Art is the therapeutic catharsis that refreshes the spirit of the creator."

My Pablo. Acrylic, 20 x 16"

Born January 1, 1933

Jennie was born in Atlanta, Georgia and grew up in Savannah. Her mother introduced Jennie and her siblings to art by taking them to a lovely cemetery in Savannah where they all were encouraged to draw the surrounding beauty. Her Korean father, a physician, also encouraged the arts. At the University of North Carolina, she majored in English and took a few art classes which re-stimulated her interest and brought forth her talent. Jennie returned home after graduation but moved back to North Carolina when she was married and started a family. She began to paint in earnest when her children were school age. She works only in watercolors because of their delicacy. Jennie has a bi-polar diagnosis. Her inner strength is not apparent on the surface because she appears to be as delicate as her painting. She is a calm, charming woman who has had the courage and endurance to suffer through 28 hospitalizations. She has now been stable for over five years with the use of suitable medication.

Memories. Watercolor, 20 x 16"

They Grew Gamboge. Watercolor, 12 x 16"

Purple Abstract. Watercolor, 30 x 22"

Vase of Patterns. Watercolor, 36 x 30"

"My main role at this time is not as an artist but as a parent and grandparent."

Fountain. Watercolor, 12 x 16"

Born August 29, 1953

Tom worked hard to become a dancer. He studied dance at Point Park College but at 19, just when he got word that he had won a spot with the Pittsburgh Ballet – his lifelong dream – he was diagnosed with bi-polar disorder and his life took an unexpected turn. Tom graduated from Scranton Preparatory School in Pennsylvania, and went on to graduate cum laude from East Straudburg University with a degree in Physical Education. He studied drama at Carnegie-Mellon University, theater at the University of Scranton and received an MA in the graduate studio art/painting program at Marywood College in Scranton. He is an art instructor, a physical education instructor, and continues with his studies at the local college. Tom has had numerous exhibits including several national exhibitions.

"I believe creativity and playfulness available through art must be taken out of the elite status and utilized in every classroom, corporate training program, rehabilitation process, and daily household activity. Only then can society at large profit from the art world in a very real way."

Anthracite 1. Mixed Media on Canvas, 10 x 13¹/₂"

"Living in Eastern PA and experiencing a landscape scarred by anthracite coal mining, I identify with an unfolding process here, where man has pulled rocks and minerals up from deep within the earth. What has been on the inside, is now on the outside."

Anthracite 2. Mixed Media on Canvas, 13¹/₂ x 10"

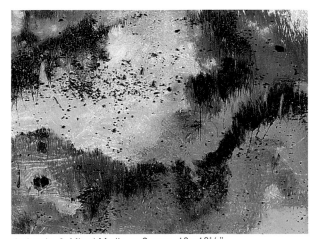

Anthracite 3. Mixed Media on Canvas, 10 x 13¹/₂"

Vesuvius. Acrylic on Canvas, 24 x 30"

Abstract. Collage/Mixed Media, 22 x 30"

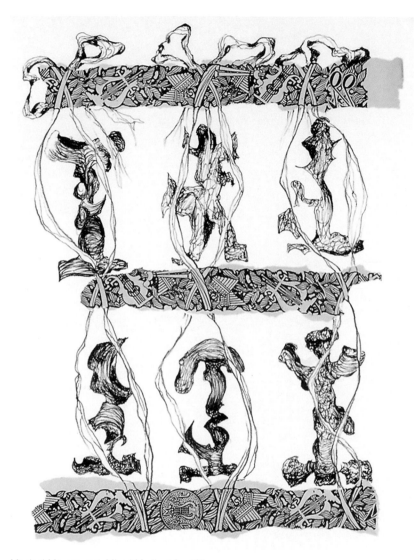

Musical Movement 1. Mixed Media, 13 x 10"

"Much of my work addresses the interaction that takes place between human and environment."

Musical Movement 2. Mixed Media, 13 x 10"

Nude. Mixed Media, 24 x 16½"

"Many of my pictures are metaphors of my combined earthliness and spirituality. They symbolize my rhythmic arrival and existence in a material world, and my concrete unity with the whirlwind of countless other humans."

Nude. Oil on Paper, 23 x 18"

63

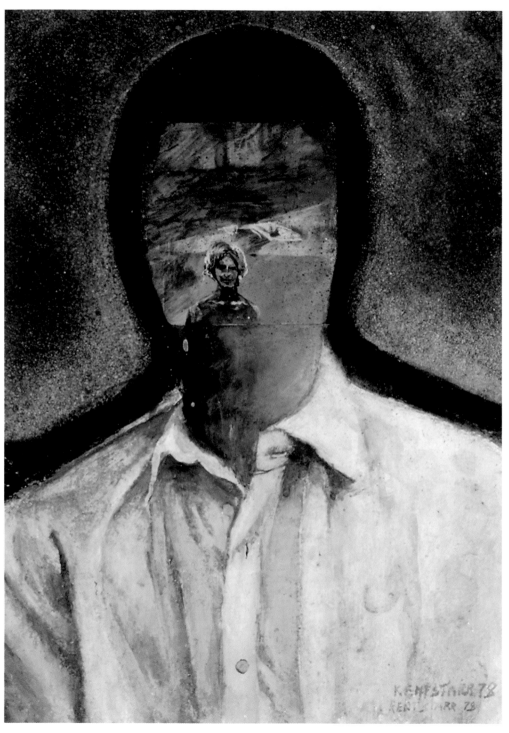

Kent has every artist's dream – a "gallery" of his own. He lives in a group home in Washington with his sketch book never far from his side. In the home, an area is set aside for "Starr's Galaxy," a showcase of his latest work. He also paints on weekends at his parent's home, experimenting with different mediums and styles. Kent became seriously interested in art while in high school in Virginia. He chose art as a career and continued his studies as a freshman at college in Tacoma, Washington until mental illness struck him at age 18. Still, art remained the one constant in his world of turmoil. He drew and sketched no matter what the illness did to him.

Born August 22, 1960

Self-Portrait. Acrylic, 13^1/$_2$ x 9^1/$_2$"

64

Yellow Barn. Acrylic, 24 x 18"

Kent has a soft spot for Kansas, having visited his grandmother many times. Barns of that area have been the subject of many of his paintings.

Black Barn. Acrylic, 12 x 12"

Birch Trees. Acrylic, 19³/₄ x 15"

Abstract. Acrylic, 12 x 10"

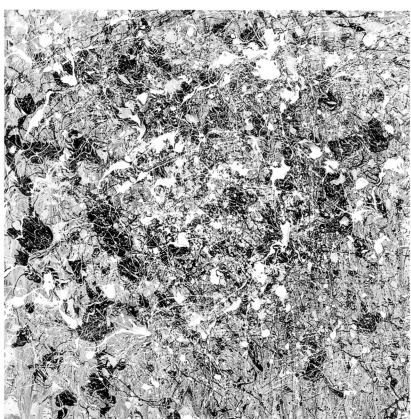

Born March 14, 1963

Michael had his first manic-depressive episode in 1982. Two years later he began painting and produced 250 paintings in a nine month manic phase. He then went into a deep and continuing depression but managed to function well enough to receive his BA in Sociology from the University of California, Santa Barbara. His abstract paintings have been featured in many galleries. He is currently working on his master's degree in clinical psychology at Antioch College in Santa Barbara.

Yellow Madness. Acrylic, 24 x 24"

Nancy's Love. Acrylic, 12 x 9"

Shades from the Universe. Acrylic, 30 x 48"

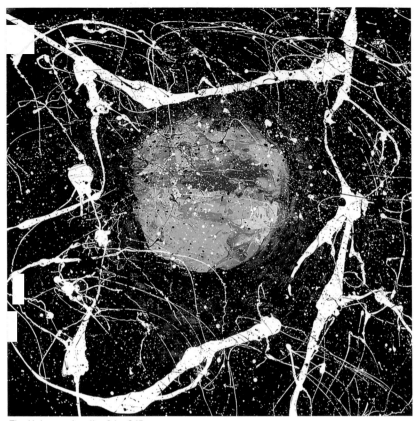

The Universe. Acrylic, 24 x 24"

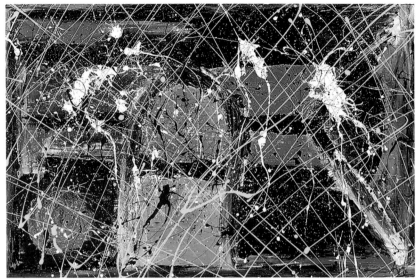

Discover the World. Acrylic, 24 x 36"

"Painting is to me a combined creative and emotional process that gives me complete freedom of expression and a chance to express the link between insanity and stability. It gives me a chance to escape the pains of human suffering and, during that time, to be lost within my own mind. For at the bottom of my soul, I see and feel with the touch of paint onto a canvas. For when I paint, I can more than anything else be myself and feel the liberty within my heart. I just wish one day I can find a place where I can feel at ease within myself and paint, not out of madness, but from tranquillity within my mind. For more than anything else in my life, I am a true artist."

"What I love is to be alone with a canvas and paints, and sometimes the pain goes away."

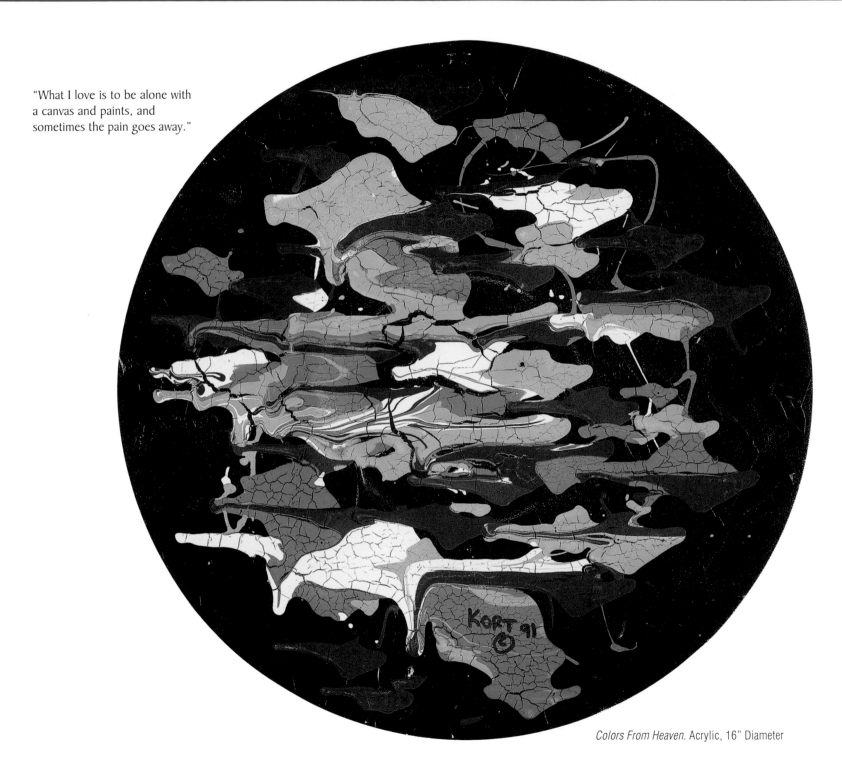

Colors From Heaven. Acrylic, 16" Diameter

71

Rainbows Show Father's Love for Your Sons. Acrylic, 24 x 24"

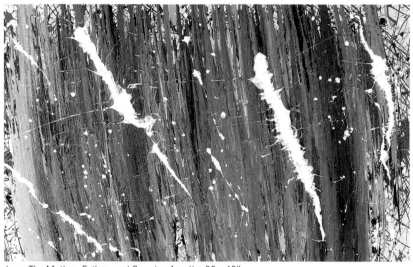

Love Thy Mother, Father, and Country. Acrylic, 30 x 48"

Sunset. Acrylic, 24 x 24"

The Inner Child. Acrylic, 24 x 24"

Born in Oahu May 28, 1945,
raised in California

Danny is a former wrestler and Vietnam veteran turned nurse, artist and poet. He turned down a full scholarship to wrestle for Cal Poly and instead attended the California College of Arts and Crafts in Oakland for one year. "I had no imagination. I needed more experience in the realities of life before continuing with my art." Joining the National Guard in 1963, he was on duty during the Watts and Berkeley riots. Danny then went into the Army, was sent to Germany and then on to Vietnam. He spent 17 months in Vietnam and in 1971, was incorrectly diagnosed with stress-related, post war syndrome nervous breakdown. Finally in 1980, he was correctly diagnosed with Bi-polar disorder. Even while working as a machinist for 19 years, Danny painted on weekends. After spending 33 years in California, he returned to Hawaii in 1982. Danny has earned two AA's in Arts and Humanities and a liberal arts degree from Kauai Community College. He has studied nursing and has earned CNA and LPN certificates. A fine spokesman for mental illness, Danny lectures on mental illness wherever and whenever asked throughout the Islands.

"I feel like I have walked through a door and I see much more clearly now. I paint with an anger and fury for all the years no one tried to help me."

Needlepoint on Maui. Acrylic, 30 x 22"

"With experience comes the visions of dreams."

Rapture. Acrylic, 20 x 16"

Lion of Judah. Acrylic, 20 x 16"

"We must work with one another and share our gifts."

Lost Heritage. Acrylic, 20 x 16"

Hootie's Family. Acrylic, 16 x 20"

"Art is my therapy."

Farewell Gauguin. Acrylic, 20 x 16"

Anahola Valley. Acrylic, 30 x 24"

Village of the Falls. Acrylic, 20 x 16"

Don't go chasing waterfalls
Unless you have a plan.
Don't go chasing waterfalls
In Peter Pan's land.
Don't go chasing waterfalls
Unless you have a plan
For you may end up alone
In Never Never land.
Don't go chasing waterfalls
Unless you have a plan....
– Danny De Leon

Born in 1989. The Host Personality was born in 1937 in New York City.

Aranda's diagnosis is Dissociative Disorder, which in her case takes the form of multiple personalities. The personality of Aranda appeared in 1989. The entire group of personalities has been under the dedicated care of a talented and patient psychiatrist. In 1987, Sondra, a child personality began to draw with felt tip pens given to her by her psychiatrist during one of the many hospitalizations. When Aranda's personality arrived she was interested in Sondra's art and began to draw the way a child does, even though she had an MA in social psychology and a BA in philosophy. Now, even though she has had no formal training, her pen and ink drawings are breathtaking in their detail and she is equally skilled in watercolor and acrylics. The group of personalities continue in treatment while living independently in an apartment in the Pacific Northwest.

Playa. Ink, 3 x 12"

Flowers. Watercolor/Ink, 9 x 13"

"When I paint I simply put my mind in neutral and begin."

Woman with Long Hair. Ink, 12 x 9"

"Nothing was ever finished, marriage, children, pilot's license, schooling, jobs. Illness wreaks havoc with life."

Thinking. Ink, 12 x 9"

Michaels

In Profile. Ink, 9 x 12"

Bifocals. Mixed Media, 10¹/₂ x 11"

Gettin¹ It On. Watercolor and Ink, 11 x 7¹/₂"

"The reason – the point – the benefit of the art is – at it's most essential level –
to enable us to endure, to go on, to keep others safe."

Time Out of Mind. Watercolor, 5³/₄ x 9¹/₂"

Woman with Bird. Ink, 5 x 2"

Slip Stitch. Graphite and Prismacolor, 14 x 11"

Punch Line. Ink, 7¹/₄ x 11¹/₂"

"The art continues to be a balm for the electrical-chemical-emotional- whatever fire storms in the brain and heart."

New Life ("Eppur Si Muove" — And Yet It Does Move). Watercolor/Ink, 8¹/₂ x 12"

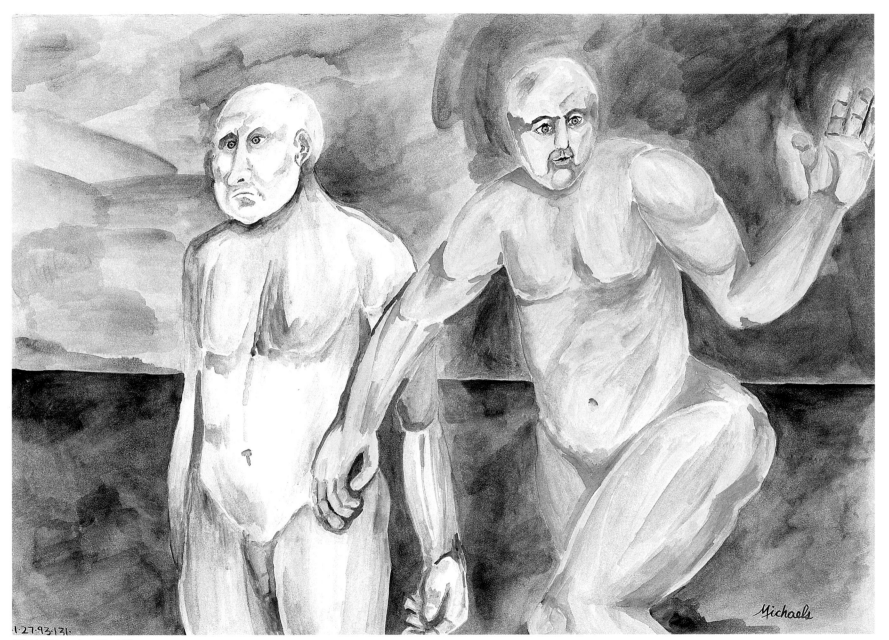

Flight. Watercolor, 10 x 14"

Born February 16, 1954

Around town in Eugene, Oregon, Eric is known as an artist, ready with a quick joke or pun. His bright paintings show an elfish, subtle humor; their titles often carry a sly, double meaning. As an artist Eric started out with etchings. When he became ill, he was studying art at Southern Oregon College. With extreme courage he overcame the "demons and the devils" that consumed his waking and sleeping life and gradually under treatment and medication a "new" Eric emerged. His love of art never swayed but the manner in which it presented itself did. His early etchings demanded a concentration and steadiness that he could no longer maintain so he turned to painting. Although Eric's life is not as he planned and he mourns that life, his family is proud of him and his rich talent.

Gargoyle. Print, 31 x 25"

Queen, King, Archangel. Print, 25 x 31"

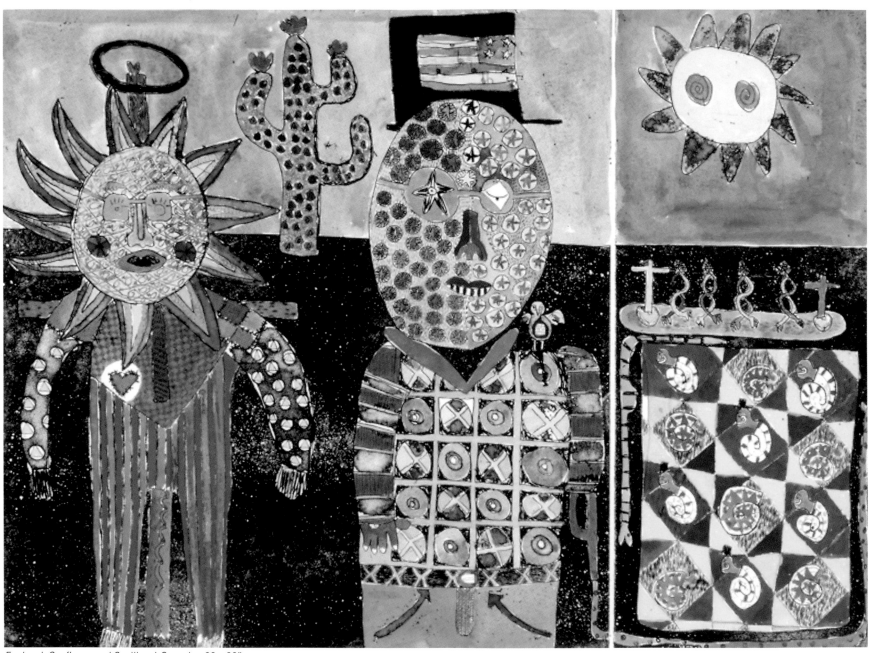

Egghead, Sunflower and Snailhead. Gouache, 22 x 30"

Swallowtail. Gouache, 24 x 18"

Eric calls his newer work "Contemporary Folk Art."

Vain Eggs. Etching/Gouache, 22 x 16"

Born June 29, 1953

Even as a child Teino knew he was different. His feelings and moods were unlike those he saw in other kids. In fact, his family history includes several manic-depressives, alcoholics and one uncle who suffered from schizophrenia. Uncle Tom was subjected to a lobotomy in the late 50's. Today Uncle Tom lives in a barred, isolated cell in a large Missouri mental institution. Teino's father was the only one who had great insight and empathy for his brother-in-law. "It is easier for most people to immobilize or lock away a problem than to try to understand the nature of the mental illness," (The Attitude Adjustment painting was done with Uncle Tom in mind). Teino eventually took his father's name of Finnish origin as his own. He says, "My father was an incredible father and a brilliant educator, who dedicated his life to helping others. My work is dedicated to him." Teino was diagnosed as being manic-depressive in 1989. During the first three years of his mania and subsequent depression he refused to take the medication required to level his moods. Only after adherence to medication has he been able to focus on his art and a job in sales.

Self-Portrait. Mixed Media, 23³/₄ x 19¹/₂"

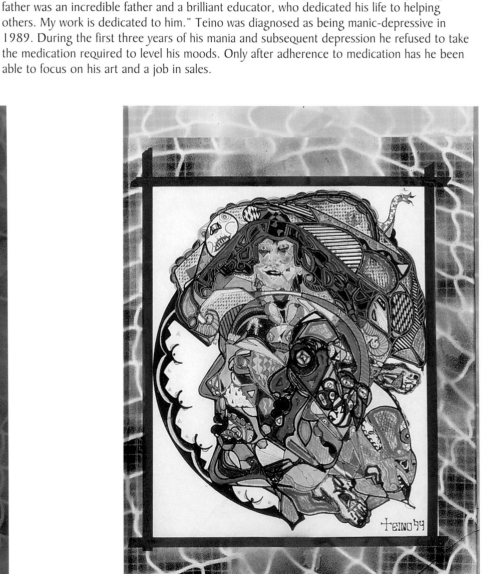

Attitude Adjustment. Mixed Media, 23¹/₂ x 17¹/₂"

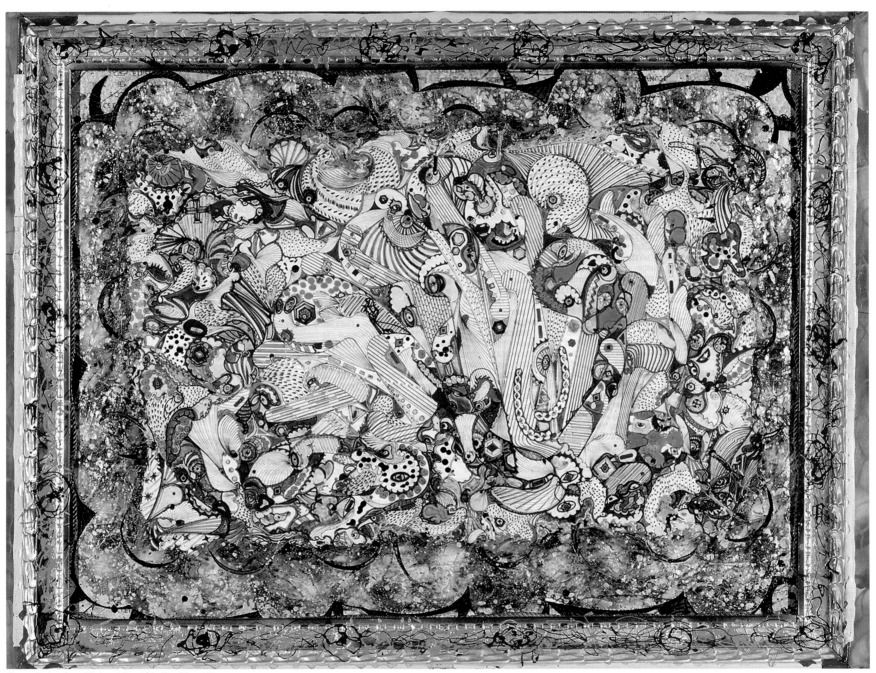

Prescription for a Vision. Mixed Media, 35 x 48"

"Manic-depression has made me a more insightful person and artist. Mind energy is different from physical energy."

Jennifer. Mixed Media, 23 1/2 x 17 3/4"

Mother's Reflection. Mixed Media, 60 x 26"

Sheba. Mixed Media/Glass, 27 x 20"

"It takes tremendous courage to wade into the public eye. The plight of the artist is many times filled with intense isolation and personal toil. This time, for me, is turned into creating art. Art allows the artist to express, feel and to heal his inner self."

"Autosymbolism is predominately my style. My only desire is to create what I feel, rather than to imitate the work of others."

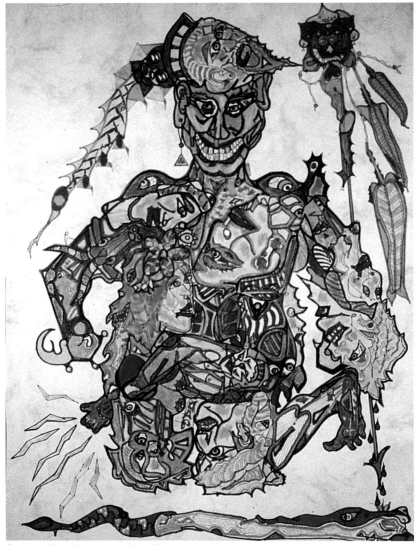

Revenge '64. Mixed Media, 30 x 26"

97

Born March 5, 1955

Catherine was always a free spirit. At age 19 she left her home in Los Angeles for Paris to "become a writer." A few years later she moved to Heidelberg, West Germany and studying at the University of Maryland overseas campus, began to paint with oils, the medium she has stuck with ever since. In West Germany she became ill and had severe emotional trauma. She returned to her family in Los Angeles. In her despondency she was unable to paint and attempted suicide. Her psychiatrist urged her to pick up a paint brush again and now Catherine's focus is on large oil paintings. She is in graduate school at Cal State University, Northridge.

"I paint every week, and, as a personal therapy to me, it is like food for the soul."

Inside My Head. Oil, 24 x 18"

Carousel. Oil, 32 x 40"

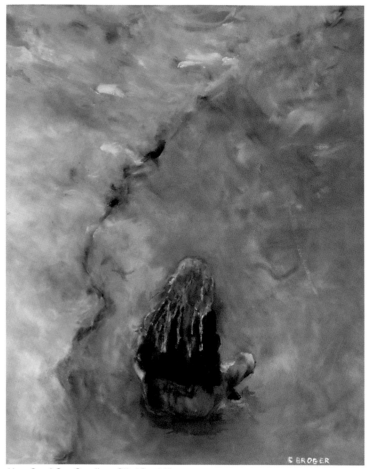

How Can I Say Goodbye. Oil, 18 x 14"

"My major art themes are life/death, emotional pain, relationships, nature, carousels (the ups and down cycle), and drug abuse."

Still Alive. Oil, 22 x 28"

Earthquake '94. Mixed Media, 24 x 48"

"My art is a true gift from God and it is ALL for me. I have shown myself and others what a person can accomplish if he really tries, regardless of handicap or illness."

Lost in the Snow. Oil, 40 x 30"

"You have to fight. You must struggle through the dark abyss 'til you are forced to see the light. Then you can also begin to create..."

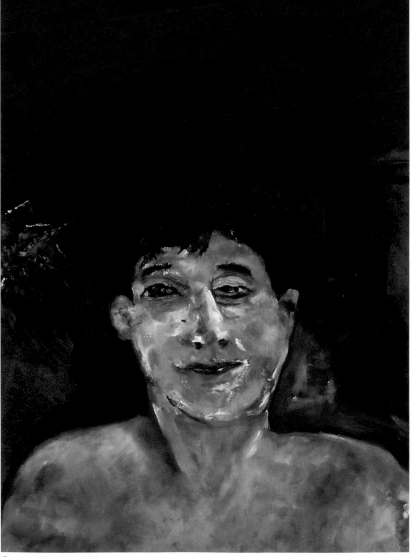

THESE BATS

There are these bats inside my soul,
I keep wishing they would go
yet they don't seem to want to leave,

they're creeping, crawling up my sleeves
they're scratching, clawing at my neck,
my head's howling in a constant wreck.

— Catherine Broger

Douglas. Oil, 24 x 20"

Lovers on Mulholland. Oil, 36 x 36"

LOVERS ON MULHOLLAND

Over the mountains, into darkness
the round, white moon
half-faced and ethereal

A hidden, black skyline
city jewels sparkling
of gold and ruby twinkling

The two lovers reveal themselves
in the scorching, night air
into each other
into the mask of eternity.
Illuminated forms of flesh,
with lit, passionate faces.

   – Catherine Broger

MARK BISHOP

Born March 24, 1959

Mark's creative spirit doesn't stop with his portrait art. He is active in theater, music, film making, video production, and writing projects. At age 10 he was a soprano in the Portland Boy's Choir and toured the western and central states in the summer. Mark staked out the back of the Greyhound bus and drew faces. He heeded the advice of his photographer father who told him that he should try to capture faces if he wanted to become an artist. Mark established his reputation at school as an artist. Later he studied art at Walla Walla College.

"I try to express myself through my art. In a way, my art is like a signature – it expresses who I am."

"My approach to drawing portraits is different than that of most artists. I look deep into the subjects faces and seek to express an aspect of myself through the portrait created."

Stir It Up. Pastel, 6 x 11¹/₂"

Black Pot. Pastel, 16 x 11¹/₂"

Java Coffee. Pastel, 16 x 11¹/₂"

"I view art as an outlet for my feelings about myself in relation to the world about me."

"My grandfather told me that when he first came to the west coast around the turn of the century, he saw black cowboys out here in Oregon."

Cowboy. Pastel, 15$\frac{1}{2}$ x 12"

105

"This is a picture of Mary in her old age, years after the ascension of Jesus. She is reflecting on the fact that Jesus is coming again and that she is the mother of the Son of Man, the name by which Jesus most desired to be called."

Mary. Pastel, 32 x 26½"

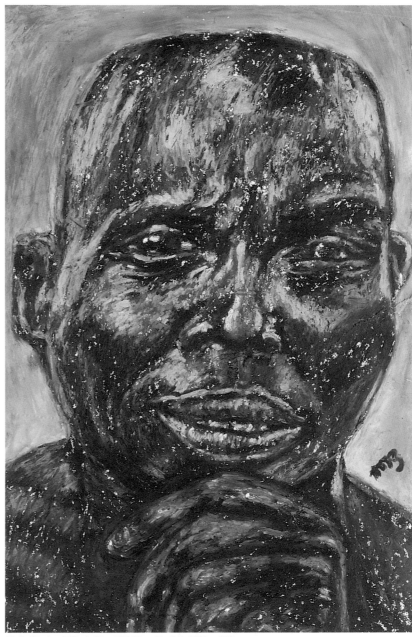

Early Study of Black Man Thinking. Pastel, 15$\frac{1}{2}$ x 12"

"The man is thinking about the goodness of life, about how God blessed him with friends, family, shelter, and clothing."

Black Man Thinking. Pastel, 61 x 36"

Born March 26, 1948

Suzanne knew by age 5 that she was going to be an artist. Both grandfathers were artists and her father drew cartoons. She earned her BA from Oshkosh University in 1980. Suzanne wanted to become a graphic artist but marriage and a child interrupted that dream. She is an avid reader with total recall, reading from one to three books per day since she was 13. Her family history dates back to the 16th century to Penelope Deveroix who married Richard Rich, first cousin of Queen Elizabeth I. She attributes many of her "quirks" or unusual "gifts" such as clairvoyance to her family lineage. Suzanne puts out a monthly newsletter of her many interests, including astrology, dance, diet, Feng Shui, and Zen. She says, "I am now turning words into art and art into words." She is also trying to loosen her tight graphic style, focusing on painting water lilies.

Fetch. Ink on Mylar, 10 x 8"

Two Persians. Watercolor, Marker, and Acrylic, 20 x 16"

"It's fun, hard work, skilled labor, manifesting dream images, intentional experimentation."

Fluff. Acrylic and Candle Dye, 14 x 18"

"Art is a series of puzzles – changing all the time."

Water Lilies. Acrylic, 18 x 24"

Night-Blooming Lilies. Oil, 16 x 28"

"I have lately been playing with light in my painting, trying to combine van Gogh's techniques while using the subjects of Monet. I am beginning to use the adult palette of changing colors to reach the spirit or essence of flowers."

Yellow is...

A beautiful warm sun.

The petals of a

Black-Eyed Susan.

Rich creamy butter.

Fall leaves fluttering

toward the ground.

Gas lamps flickering

on a long deserted street.

But most of all, yellow is

A warm loving color

That assures us that

Another day will come.

David Lambert

1978

at age 11

NARSAD Artworks is an all volunteer nonprofit corporation which incorporates art created by persons suffering from severe mental illness into products such as note and holiday cards sold nationally for the benefit of the mentally ill. These products are sold through affiliates of the National Alliance for the Mentally Ill, the National Depressive and Manic-Depressive Association, the National Mental Health Association and other selected outlets.

The NARSAD Artworks program benefits persons with mental illness by:
- Educating the public about mental illness
- Creating self-esteem for artists and those near them
- Raising funds for local groups and research
- Providing income to artists and other consumers
- Fighting stigma by providing a new and positive image of persons who suffer from mental illness.

All NARSAD Artworks are created by artists who have or have had a mental illness. They are paid at prevailing commercial rates but, unlike commercial firms, their art is returned after processing and all rights are returned later. Packaging is done by mentally ill persons in paid work rehabilitation.

NARSAD Artworks has become the nation's clearing house for art created by persons with mental illness. It is becoming increasingly used as cover art and in educational and product brochures as well as in NARSAD Artworks products.

NARSAD, the National Alliance for Research on Schizophrenia and Depression, was founded by the National Alliance for the Mentally Ill, the National Depressive and Manic Depressive Association and the National Mental Health Association in 1986. It is now the largest public contributor supported funder of research in neurobiological disorders in the world. NARSAD's principal program is the selection and funding of grants to young scientists. Its Established Investigator program provides research awards to senior scientists on a highly selective basis for outstanding, innovative, and urgent research projects.

NARSAD has provided 1,378 grants to 739 scientists. These grants were given to scientists in 117 universities and medical research institutions, predominantly in the United States. Recipients are also in Canada, Sweden, Switzerland, France, Israel, Germany, England, and Italy.

Mental illness research is important because:
- In any six-month period, one in every five adult Americans, more than 30 million people, suffers from a diagnosable mental disorder
- 17.3 million Americans suffer from severe mental illness
- A fourth of all hospital beds in this country are occupied by people with mental illness – more than those occupied by patients with heart disease, cancer, and respiratory illness combined
- 35 percent of homeless people are mentally ill, suffering primarily from schizophrenia or depression
- more than 7 million children and adolescents suffer from mental illness
- more than 35,000 Americans commit suicide every year – an average of once every 15 minutes.

NARSAD Artworks

P.O. Box 941 • La Habra, California • (800) 607-2599

NARSAD

60 Cutter Mill Road • Great Neck, NY 11021 • (516) 829-0091

The severe mental illnesses are biomedical puzzles, which affect many human functions, including the thought processes in the schizophrenias and the moods and emotions in depression and manic-depression.
For more information contact:

NMHA (National Mental Health Association)
1021 Prince Street • Alexandria, Virginia 22314 • (703) 684-7722
Mission: Public Education, Services and Advocacy

OCD (Obsessive-Compulsive Disorder Foundation, Inc.)
P.O. Box 70 • Milford, Connecticut 06460 • (203) 878-5669
Mission: Self-help and Advocacy

NAMI (National Alliance for the Mentally Ill)
200 North Glebe Road, #1015 • Arlington, Virginia 22203 • (800) 950-6264
Mission: Family Support and Advocacy

NDMDA (National Depressive & Manic-Depressive Association)
730 North Franklin Street, #501 • Chicago, Illinois 60610 • (800) 826-3632
Mission: Self-help and Advocacy